D0604353

FOCUSED
YOUR FUTURE STARTS NOW!

FOCUSED
YOUR FUTURE STARTS NOW!

JASON KIESAU

Book Press™
publishing

Published in Des Moines, Iowa, by BookPress Publishing.

Publisher's Cataloging-in-Publication Data

Kiesau, Jason.
    Focused : Your Future Starts Now! / Jason Kiesau.
    pages cm
    ISBN 978-0-9862416-4-2
    Includes bibliographical references.

1. Success. 2. Young adults—Conduct of life. 3. Youth—Conduct of life.
4. Attitude (Psychology). I. Title.

BJ1661 .K49 2015
646.7 --dc23   2015943995

First Edition

Printed in the United States of America
10 9 8 7 6 5 4 3 2 1

This book was written in the memory of my oldest sister Jodi,
who lost her battle with cancer on January 29, 2014. She was
good to everyone, the nucleus of our family, and someone I
never wanted to disappoint. Her spirit lives in everything I do.

The completion of this project is dedicated to my mother,
June Kiesau, and my children, Marriah and Daxon.
Mom, I owe you. Things weren't always easy and I certainly
didn't help, but your commitment to family never wavered.
Thank you for never giving up and always supporting me.
Marriah and Daxon, words can't express the purpose I feel
as your dad. You two inspire me in so many ways. I want
you to believe in yourselves, focus on the right things for
the right reasons, and follow your dreams. I love you,
and can't wait to see how you impact the world.

CONTENTS

ACKNOWLEDGMENTS

We are all products of our past, and I don't know if there is enough space to give credit to all the people who had an impact on me over the years. To all my friends and family who supported me throughout the years, even when you weren't sure if I knew what I was doing. To all my teachers who made education as much about life as a GPA. To all my professors who took the time to understand what I wanted and guided me in that direction. To my former managers who gave me opportunities to succeed and fail, allowing me to develop and sharpen the skills necessary to accomplish my goals. To mentors over the years who shared time, experience, and expertise. To the entire Merit leadership team for the stability, support, and opportunities that have allowed me to confidently live my life and pursue my passions.

Thank you! Life is good!

CHAPTER 1

My Reality Check

It was March 2001. I was 23 and was sitting by the phone in my bedroom at my parents' house in Cedar Rapids, Iowa. I was expecting a call from the Creative Director with the NBA's Charlotte Hornets about a graphic design position I interviewed for the week before.

Two months before my interview with them, I had my one year review for my first job out of college. I was a graphic designer at an ad agency, and some may have described me as a little too confident and ignorant for my own good. Going into the review my expectations were to go in and receive praise, get my 3% raise, and walk out feeling happy. Ignorant for sure! In reality, my boss told me things weren't working out, and he gave me three options that had nothing to do with me continuing to work there.

My options:

> We could part ways on the spot and I could go home, and receive pay for two weeks.

> I could put in my two week notice and they could "release me" on the spot so it appeared it was my decision and I was moving on.

I could put in my two week notice and I could continue to work over the next two weeks.

Once I finished crying, he told me I could go home, think about it, and let him know. I chose option three. My ego was shattered, but even with my level of ignorance at that time, I knew the right thing to do was to finish my work over the next two weeks and leave them in the best spot I could. On my last day, I remember my boss brought me in his office and praised me for the character I showed given the situation. It meant a lot back then and has stuck with me today. Thank you, Mark! Fourteen years later, I am still grateful for the leadership my boss exhibited and how he handled that situation. I did not deserve it.

Sometime over the course of my final two weeks with the ad agency, I was sitting at my computer and heard the familiar "You Have Mail" notification from my AOL email account. It was an email from the Creative Director with the Charlotte Hornets of the National Basketball Association (NBA). He said someone had sent him my website and my design skills impressed him. Based on the sports focus in my design portfolio, he thought I'd be interested in their open position. He was right; I was very interested.

I spent February of 2001 going through the Hornets' recruiting and hiring process. I had phone interviews, completed design projects they loved, and finally flew to Charlotte to meet the design team and interview with members of leadership. After arriving in Charlotte, I had dinner with the design team and we wrapped up the night with a late night tour of the Hornets' corporate office. I remember feeling confident and building great rapport. At some point I asked him what he thought. His reply: "If nothing disastrous happens we will probably offer you the position tomorrow." The job was mine, and I was on cloud nine.

Though no official offer was made at that time, they told me to expect a call by the end of the week. But the call never came.

Almost an entire week after I was supposed to hear from them, I got an email from the Creative Director. Do you want to guess what the email said?

"Dear Jason,

Thank you for your interest in employment with the Charlotte Hornets. Though we enjoyed learning about you, we have decided to go in another direction . . ."

Another direction? Say what?

After the initial confusion, anger, sadness, and self-pity wore off, I picked up the phone and called him. When he answered, my emotions were clear, yet I was able to stay professional. He seemed a little uncomfortable as well. I expressed my confusion because everything appeared to be moving in the right direction. He explained I said something during the tour that concerned him, something that made him question my attitude and work ethic.

I remember the moment like it was last night. It was around 9PM, and we were walking through the creative area within the Hornets' headquarters. He was explaining their design-to-print process. It was different and far less cumbersome than what I was used to at the ad agency, and I celebrated that while letting him know what I did not like about my old process.

And that was it. My celebration mixed with my remarks about the old process made him question whether I was the right person. He decided that I was not. When he told me what cost me the job, all I could do was shake my head.

That was the moment that changed everything. That rejection was the "kick in the balls" that finally dropped me and had me questioning whether I was going to be able to get up.

This was my Identity Crisis.

That night, my mind was going crazy as I lay in my bed, reflecting back on my entire world and questioning everything. I thought about childhood, how I grew up, and all the mistakes that I made. I had to come to terms with the fact that not only did I lose my first job out of college, but I screwed up the chance at a dream job, all in a span of eight weeks. I remember wondering if I was destined to be a screw-up and whether things would ever be good enough. I came to the conclusion that either life was supposed to be a struggle or something needed to be learned. Option one didn't sound good, so I accepted that something needed to be learned.

At that moment I made a commitment to learn and listen. I put myself on a mission to understand success and characteristics of successful people. The mistakes and struggles were tiring and I wanted a successful and fulfilling life. I had no choice.

I spent the next four months working full time at a copy shop and saving money in preparation to move to Des Moines and go back to school. In August of 2001, two weeks before my 24th birthday, I packed up all my stuff, moved out of my mom's basement, and started back to school in Des Moines. Two of my first classes were Sociology and Psychology of Success, which fit the new mission I was on. Both classes challenged me to think about myself and the world around me in new and exciting ways. Throughout that first semester, I couldn't get enough of this stuff and I could feel myself changing as I continued to learn about success.

The cherry on the sundae came when I was in Target one day looking at books and I decided to buy *The Seven Habits of Highly Effective People*, by Stephen Covey. I didn't know anything about Stephen Covey or his book, but something about it appealed to me. I wanted to understand success and the characteristics of success and the title made me feel like it aligned well with my mission.

That book changed my life.

When I finished *The Seven Habits of Highly Effective People* and all the exercises in it, I knew I wanted to spend my life coaching, counseling, teaching, training, or speaking. I wanted to help people experience the personal growth I was experiencing. I grew up wanting to teach elementary school and the book helped me reconnect with who I was and what I was passionate about–helping people. It challenged me to identify my values, set my standards, and create a vision and plan based on those values and standards.

In a matter of six months, I went from a scared 23-year

old to a revived 24-year old who wanted to change the world. The only problem: I wasn't sure how. At that time I only had an associate's degree in Visual Communications, and zero experience coaching, counseling, teaching, training, and speaking. Outside of my teachers, I didn't know anyone who was doing what I wanted to spend my life doing. My vision made me realize that I had a lot of work to do if I was going to have the life I wanted.

I was up for the challenge and put myself on a five-year plan. I set the goal that by 30 I would be coaching, counseling, teaching, training, or speaking. It was at that moment my "By 30 Vision" was born.

I spent the next five years committed to working my "By 30 Vision" plan. I continued to self-study. I went back to school and completed my BA in Organizational Management and Communication, all while working full-time in positions that either aligned with or helped me learn skills that supported my success. In 2006, three months after I turned 29, I accepted a position as Business Coach with E-Myth Iowa, where I worked with small business owners all over the country helping them connect their businesses with their values and passion.

YES! I achieved my "By 30 Vision," and what I learned through that process has been the foundation for everything else I have done in my life: parenting, serving my community, and managing our training department at work.

As I got older, I realized I was studying and practicing leadership the whole time. The challenge I gave myself from the age of 24 to 30 is the same challenge every leader faces, whether it's leading themselves or a Fortune 500 company. And this is the opportunity you have in this book: to lead yourself and confidently pursue the life you deserve.

When you finish this book, my hope is that two things will happen for you:

- You have a clear vision for what you want your life to look like in five years. I know that might sound kind of heavy right now, but roll with it. I'm going to walk you through the discovery process step by step.

- You have the confidence to make it a reality. If you haven't figured this out, you soon will. Lots of people talk about what they want in their lives. Few people do it. I don't want you to be a talker. I want you to be a doer, and to be a doer you need to have confidence in what you are doing. Don't worry; I'm going to help you with that, too.

Your 20's are or will be the most important years of your life. A successful mentor of mine is often asked how he reached so much success at such a young age. His response, "I didn't waste my 20's." Think about what the world expects of you. When you graduated high school you were forced to decide what you would do the rest of your life. Between the ages of 18 and 25, you are expected to make major life decisions that will impact you forever; decisions that may lead you to a life of opportunity or struggle, happiness or frustration, meaning or regret.

CHAPTER 2

Escaping the Maze

If I polled every 21-year-old in the United States and asked if they thought they were going to have a life of happiness or a life of struggle, I bet 99% would say they will have a life of happiness. But take a look around; that definitely is not reality.

Our entire lives we get force-fed this one-size fits all, cookie cutter "road map of success" that goes something like:

- Follow directions, behave, and get good grades so you can go to a good college

- Get good grades in college so you can graduate and get a "good job" (as defined by society or those with whom you associate)

- Get a good job

- Meet your life partner, get married, have kids

- Cars, Houses, Big Screen TV's, and more and more and more stuff

- Live, work, and be happy

When I was finishing my undergraduate degree, I was working and going to school full-time. I felt like I was in an always changing, never-ending maze, doing a good job at work, doing enough to get by in school, and having an awesome social life. Oh… and I should probably mention sleep in there. Finding time for sleep is pretty important.

Some of you know exactly what I'm talking about because you are either in that boat now or you were in the boat within the past few years. Isn't it fun trying to manage all this stuff while trying to meet your professors' expectations, not disappoint your parents, and keep your friends happy? And for what…some kind of society-defined fantasy life telling us that if we do the right things our lives will be great?

So, what if you don't follow the plan? If you don't follow the plan, the world looks at you like you're lost and falling behind. This can take a toll on your self-worth and self-confidence.

The fact is that maze you are in doesn't go away just because you finish college. Without knowing it, most of you will or have been led into a bigger maze our parents like to refer to as the Real World–a maze that is more complex and less forgiving, a maze where a few wrong moves may send you down a path in the opposite direction of where you thought you were going.

I don't dislike the plan on the previous page because it's a "bad plan." I dislike the plan because we're made to believe we are wrong or falling behind if we don't follow it exactly. The challenging part is that many people follow it and expect it to bring them happiness, success, and fulfillment. It doesn't just happen; you must modify the plan and adapt it to your values, passions, and standards. Some people blindly follow along and do whatever the rest of the world tells them to do, without considering what is right for them. Once reality hits them, they start to question who they are and what they are doing. This isn't a bad thing if this leads them to a place of clarity and connection, but many times it leads them to a place of anxiety, insecurity, and frustration. For some people, that never goes away. I call this the *identity crisis*.

What's an identity crisis?

You're probably wondering, "What the hell is an identity crisis?"

I'll answer in a moment, but first, I have a few questions: Is the real world like you thought it would be? Are you who you thought you would be? Are you where you thought you would be in the following areas: Health, Finances, Relationships, Career, Fun, and Impact?

An identity crisis is defined as "a period of uncertainty and confusion in which a person's sense of identity becomes insecure, typically due to a change in their expected aims or role in society."[1] When we aren't going in the direction we thought we would be (expected aim), and we are not living the lives we desire (expected role in society), we experience confusion and insecurity.

We all have interests and passions, goals, and expectations for ourselves and our lives. What happens when we realize we aren't living out our passions and interests? How do we feel when we aren't achieving our goals and aspirations? What do we do when we aren't meeting our own expectations?

Are we excited about the world? Are we living with passion, meaning, and purpose? No. Instead, we experience an identity crisis.

I think everyone experiences this for a few reasons.

Relative Deprivation Theory

In his book, *David and Goliath*, Malcolm Gladwell talks about relative deprivation theory. In a nutshell, relative deprivation theory says that we do not build our view of ourselves based on our actual standing in the world. Instead, our view of ourselves is based on how we compare to the people in our social circles. Our motivation, persistence, and confidence will be determined by how we see ourselves within those groups. If we feel good about our place in the group, we are confident. If we don't feel good about our place in the group, we are in trouble. Gladwell explains further in this excerpt from a speech he gave at Google-sponsored ZietgeistMinds in 2013[2]:

> I think it is because as human beings, we dramatically underestimate the costs of being at the bottom of a hierarchy... this exceedingly robust phenomenon which says that as human beings, we do not form our self-assessments based on our standing in the world. We form our self-assessments based on our standing in our immediate circle, on those in the same boat as ourselves, right? So a classic example of relative deprivation theory is which kind of country—which countries have the highest suicide rates? Happy countries or unhappy countries? And the answer is happy countries. If you are morbidly depressed in a country where

everyone else is really unhappy, you don't feel that unhappy. right? You are not comparing yourself to the universe — the whole universe of people out there. No. You are comparing yourself to your neighbors and the kids at school and they are unhappy, too, so you are sort of fine. But if you are morbidly depressed in a country where everyone is jumping up and down for joy, you are really depressed, right? That is a very, very, very profoundly serious place to be and so as a result, you get that sad outcome more often.

His following statement says it all: "When it comes to confidence and motivation and self-efficacy, the things that really matter when it comes to making your way in the world, relative position matters more than absolute position." To sum it up: people compare themselves to everyone around them because that's all they know to compare themselves to. The identity crisis comes when people's lives don't meet their expectations which are shaped by the culture around them.

Negativity Bias

We have a "negativity bias." In the Tracom Group's program titled *Adaptive Mindset for Resiliency*[3], they state that we are hard-wired to focus on negative, unpleasant information compared to positive information.

- In one study, researchers showed participants positive, negative, and neutral stimuli and found that electrical activity in the cerebral cortex was strongest in response to negative stimuli, indicating we are wired to focused on the negative.

- The negativity bias is even evident in our language. For example, of the 558 emotion words in the U.S. English Dictionary, 62% of them are negative and only 38% of are positive. Of the most common words people use, 70% of them are negative. This means that we have a more complex and varied way of conceptualizing negative feelings compared to positive feelings.

Tracom Group continues: "This negativity bias has a strong influence over us. Even when we experience a lot of positive events in our day, one negative event can dramatically alter our mood. Negative events are more likely to draw our attention and have a stronger, more long-lasting impact on us. This negativity bias means we often feel overwhelmed by challenges, we see threats where none exist, and we fail to see opportunity in adversity. In short, the negativity bias keeps us from being as resilient as we can be."

Dysfunctional Attractiveness of Regrets

I think there is something dysfunctional and dramatically attractive about having regrets and playing the "woulda, coulda, shoulda" game. Feeling sorry for ourselves gives us meaning and attention. It's easier to look in the mirror with our negativity bias and try to validate or make excuses for why life isn't how we want it to be than it is to see the positives and opportunities we have around us.

Our Consumerism Culture

I think the clutter of our consumerism culture primes us for an identity crisis. According to CASRO (Council of American Survey Research Organizations), spending on marketing research in the United States has reached $6.7 Billion. If you look at spending worldwide, it is closer to $18.9 Billion.[4] This means the business world is spending billions and billions of dollars to make sure they understand how we think, behave, and how we are motivated so they can manipulate their messages and presentations in ways to make us take action. This means we receive tens of thousands of messages every single day trying to influence us to do something. They know the only way to influence us is to create emotion that is linked to either fear or opportunity.

We are at a disadvantage. The business world knows more about you and I than we know about ourselves. It knows more about our parents and siblings and future children than we ever will and all they care about is selling them a product or service.

Advertising is all about creating pain and insecurity within its audience. Take a moment to listen to the advertisements you hear on the radio and see on the TV or Internet. We are bombarded with thousands and thousands of messages and information every single day.

- How many of the messages are positive?
- How many of the messages are productive?

- What percentage of them are making you a better person?

- How many of the messages have your best interest in mind?

- What are you listening to?

- What do you focus on?

- Do they enable your insecurities?

- Do they make you more confident?

They are either telling you that you're not good enough or selling you on the fantasy of how things can be better. We change our lives for two reasons: to avoid pain or pursue opportunity. The business world understands this and they are experts at pulling your strings. Don't get me wrong, there are some great products and services out there, but their # 1 goal is for you to buy their stuff. And I'm OK with you buying their stuff, but do it confidently on your terms, not theirs.

Our consumerism culture wants us to experience an Identity Crisis. It needs us to. It's good for business. The more uncertainty, confusion, and insecurity we feel, the more money we will spend trying to fix it. They know this and the sooner you realize this, the better.

Everyone experiences an identity crisis at some point in their lives, and everyone reacts differently to the experience. For some, it's a wake-up call that motivates them to make positive changes that lead to meaning and purpose. For others, it's a nightmare that impacts their self-worth and quality of life for the rest of their lives.

A lot of people experience it right before they turn thirty years old because they aren't where they thought they would be. When I was VP of Professional Development with the Young Professionals Connection, an organization in Des Moines that caters to young professionals between the ages of 20 and 35, I talked to lawyers who were in a funk because they weren't passionate about what they were doing. Most of them were only lawyers because that's what others in their family did and it was expected. A friend's break-up with a boyfriend shattered her world because she expected to be married and have children by now. I dated a girl whom I took to dinner for her 28th birthday, and the entire dinner she was expressing her angst about how she thought her life would be very different. She said, "I'm almost thirty, and what do I have to show for it?" Another colleague of mine appeared to have it together, but in his mid-20's experienced an identity crisis and he spun out of control with drugs and booze. Even into his mid-30's, he publicly burned bridges and ruined the positive reputation he worked hard to create.

While experiencing your identity crisis, it can feel like everyone has expectations for you and you don't want to disappoint them. If your loved ones aren't understanding or supportive, conversations with them can be frustrating and make you feel worse.

When I was 24, we celebrated my dad's last birthday. I had just started studying success and was growing and changing and my family didn't understand it. They were used to a certain identity I had. I didn't feel like they supported me, and I felt judged and frustrated. I remember going on the attack and telling people what they were doing wrong and what they needed to change. It made me question the changes I was making. Thankfully, I kept moving forward and over time they saw the man I was becoming.

My mother admits that when I was in my early 20's and on this success mission, she wasn't sure if I was going in the right direction. She didn't get it. I was doing a lot of things she couldn't relate to. What I was doing was not the map of success she had learned. Finally in my early 30's, she shared with me that at some point she realized that I was going to do what I wanted regardless of what anybody said. She felt the only way I was going to learn was by falling down and getting back up. She was right, but what she didn't understand was the fuel and motivation I had as a result of my identity crisis.

My spirit had been revived and I was on a mission.

If you look back over the course of human history, no significant changes have ever taken place without a little bit of conflict and chaos beforehand. Accept your identity crisis. Use it as a wake-up call to start paying closer attention to what really fires you up in the world and the steps you need to take to create the life you want. My life isn't perfect and I accept that, but it doesn't get me down. I love the world around me. I see nothing but opportunity around me. I attribute this attitude to focusing on the right things: my values, passions, standards, and engagement in things that are meaningful to me. Have I gone off course? Hell yes! Have

I failed? Definitely!

There is a quote that I love; in my mind, it is all about attitude:

"I never lose. I win or I learn."
- Anonymous

Your attitude is everything; your identity crisis can be the cause of great stress in your life or it can be the fuel and motivation that lead to the life you want.

CHAPTER 3

Shifting Out of Survival Mode

Some people feel the only purpose in life is to survive–we are here and we live until we don't. They simply exist and just go through the motions with no meaning, no purpose, and they are just doing what they need to do to get by and live, and they don't even realize it.

This lack of purpose and meaning impacts everything around them. They are disengaged, unfulfilled, unhappy, and depressed. They lack direction, self-confidence, and self-worth. They make decisions based on fear and pain avoidance rather than their values, passions, meaning, and purpose. They are rarely happy and fulfilled, because they don't know what truly makes them happy. They feel stuck.

Maybe they experienced things throughout their life that got them off track, wore them down, or broke them. Maybe they weren't brought up with productive messaging from those around them. Perhaps they are repeating a cycle they learned growing up. Perhaps they are just following someone else's plan.

Whatever the reasons, there are too many talented people who don't know what talents they have and don't have the confidence to get what they want. That's a tragedy. There are so many good things about the world, and when people are in survival mode they may not be able to see it.

Throughout my life I have gone through a number of phases that shaped my identity at the time. When I was little, I loved Superman and Dukes of Hazzard. When I was in the third grade, I started watching WWF and became a little Hulkamaniac. In the sixth grade, when WWF was no longer cool, I was all about professional sports like the NFL and NBA; and though I was a fat white kid I wanted to be like Bo Jackson and Michael Jordan.

This identity stayed pretty consistent through my high school years, but my sophomore year things started changing. I started my sophomore year of high school in the fall of 1992, and a few months later Dr. Dre's "The Chronic" album was released. It was the introduction of Snoop Doggy Dog and their megahit song "Nothing But a G Thang." This was part of a movement taking place (at 37 years old, I still love that song).

It felt like almost overnight a group of guys in my class, many of whom I was friends with, went from wearing Nike warm-ups and the latest pair of Jordan's to dressing like thugs with their khaki suits and sagging pants. Their identities changed and mine was challenged. I flirted with the identity change, but it just wasn't me. I didn't fit in, and, in hindsight, I'm thankful for that. Over the next couple of years I heard stories of smoking weed and drinking, breaking into houses, and fights that took place because someone looked at them the wrong way or said the wrong thing.

I always had a lot of friends, but I remember feeling lost. I couldn't relate to the wanna-be gangsters, cowboys, or preps. I felt like a nomad that just wandered; I had friendships in each group, but never felt like part of one.

Before I go any further, let me make one important point that shines some light on what you've just read. I was a follower my whole life. I didn't have the confidence to lead or set my own direction. If I tried, I would quickly concede if another person pushed harder. I was at the mercy of those around me, and this ruled me in so many ways. I didn't focus on school like I should have; I got into trouble because I was going along with the wrong people; and I never took a stand for what I thought was right. I simply wasn't confident with myself.

When I started college, I saw it as an opportunity to be confident and establish my identity. It was a game changer socially and academically. I was beginning to take control of the identity I wanted. At some point we are all faced with opportunities. The question is, when?

Everything I just talked about has played a role in what kind of man I am today, for better or for worse. We are who we are today because of our history. Our entire lives we have been charged with meeting expectations of the world around us: our parents, extended family, teachers, coaches, friends, and on a much more massive scale, our society and culture as a whole. Many of those expectations and pressures have led us to the lives we have today; the good, bad, and the ugly.

Today, you are making decisions based on who you have been molded to become. Who you are today may not be who you are meant to be. Who you are today may not be who you want to be. The influence of your parents, teachers, and friends has brought you this far, but it may not get you the life you want.

At some point, something is going to happen that will make us question who we are and the direction we are going. We can ignore it and keep doing what we've been doing only to have it resurface at a later time. Or, we can shift out of survival mode and listen to the questions that arise within us.

CHAPTER 4

Cultivating Confidence

Self-Awareness

Self-Awareness is the exact opposite of an Identity Crisis. While an Identity Crisis is insecurity in relation to whom and where we thought we would be, self-awareness is knowing who we are, where we are going, and having a plan to get there. There is no uncertainty or confusion because how we organize our lives is based on our values, passions, and vision. Above all else, self-awareness might be the most important skill to cultivate. I define it as:

- Knowing who you are
    - Values – What is important and meaningful?
    - Standards – What do you expect of yourself and the world around you?
    - Passions – What excites you about the world?
    - Goals & Dreams – What do you really want to do?
- Knowing where you are going
    - Vision – What do you want your life to look like?

- Goals – What do you need to accomplish to fulfill your vision?

- Plan – What is your plan to accomplish your goals and vision?

Every young adult in their early to mid-20's thinks they know everything. I get it. I was there. We are adults and we want to exercise our freedom and independence. The better we know who we are, where we are going, and how we are going to get there, the more we will eliminate a lot of the uncertainty and confusion that leaves people feeling insecure and stuck in Survival Mode.

Self-Respect & Self-Worth

When you look in the mirror, what do you see? When you think about your life and what you want out of it, what do you feel?

Are you motivated or discouraged?

I think it's easy for people at any age to question themselves. You've been force-fed rules and expectations your whole life, and now as an adult you have a whole new picture of what success in life looks like. You might just be getting started, but it can easily feel like you are falling behind, especially if your friends and peers appear to be in a better spot.

In late 2014, I facilitated training for a client of mine in Atlanta, Georgia. When I finished, a man from the audience stuck around and waited to chat. There was a point in my training that I talked about stress and stress management, and that resonated with him. Early in our conversation I asked how old he was and the second I did was the second he lost eye contact with me and shame came over his face. He whispered that he was 40, but no one he works with knows his age because he doesn't feel good about his position. I started asking questions and noticed he constantly compared himself to three friends and his brother. He had very little self-respect and self-worth, and he never will unless he takes ownership of it and stops comparing himself to the world around him. Before I left I gave him my card and told him to email me if he needed anything. I have yet to receive an email. I hope he is doing better. Seeing stuff like that breaks my heart.

I can empathize with his insecurities. I finished my associate's degree when I was 21. Eight months after graduation, I accepted a graphic design position making $11 per hour. I had one friend who was an engineer, making $50,000 per year. Another buddy was second in command at his dad's construction company and was making good money. Another was just starting law school.

Though I had pride in finishing school and the work I was doing, it was hard not to feel a little inferior to my friends and it impacted my confidence and worth inside our group. Now, this point in my life was before my Identity Crisis at 24, and today I see the flaws in my attitude. I put too much value on money and external things and it was impacting my self-respect and self-worth.

Growing up it is beat in to our heads the importance of having respect for people and things, and the better we are able to do this, the easier life can be. However, I don't remember at any point in my life being taught that the first person I needed to respect was myself. Yes, I was probably more insecure than the average kid, but I was so busy trying to be good for everyone else and seeking approval and validation that I never even thought about what I deserved. As a result, I was very amiable with the world around me. Most of the time I just went with the flow and I was never too assertive. If I felt what I was going to say or do was going to hurt or upset someone, I didn't say it, even when I was in the right or at a disadvantage. I didn't understand self-respect and self-worth. I put the rest of the world first.

Understanding self-respect and self-worth is our best defense against the world around us. They protect your self-esteem, confidence, and attitude.

The concept of self-respect and self-worth is such a big deal to me that we have signs hanging in our kids' rooms that I called the Rules of the House. If you ask my six-year old what self-respect means, he will tell you things like "being good to yourself," or "not saying you are dumb or stupid," or "not letting other people put you down." That's a good start. People who understand self-respect and self-worth are more confident and less likely to tolerate being bullied by people or the world around them.

Self-Confidence

Up to this point in the book I have been trying to remind you of key concepts that are critical to confidently thriving in your 20's, 30's, and beyond. And to do that, you need self-confidence. Self-confidence is the opposite of insecurity.

What is confidence? I think this 2013 article from Huffington Post[5] sums it up nicely:

> *"Owning it.*
>
> *When you're "owning it," it means that you're totally and completely at peace with who you are in every moment, interaction and experience. You make no apologies for being awkward, nervous, excited, loud, soft spoken or other... you're just you.*
>
> *You radiate charismatic energy whether or not you have an extroverted personality because you are genuinely content with yourself and your present experience."* [1]

I look at confidence and insecurity as two different roads going to the same destination.

The Confident Road

The confident road is smooth and efficient. It's a beautiful day and the driving conditions are perfect. The cruise control is set, windows are down, and your favorite song is on the radio. Your passengers are great company and everyone you encounter is friendly. You reach your destination with no problems because the directions and signs are clear. You arrive feeling great, without a worry in the world.

The Insecure Road

The insecure road is not smooth and efficient. There are

times when the days are beautiful and conditions are perfect, but they can quickly and violently change leaving you looking for a ditch or an overpass for protection. The road is winding and bumpy, changes directions frequently, and the signs are not always clear or accurate. The people you encounter are not always friendly or helpful, and your passengers are "backseat drivers," frequently criticizing and making you second guess where you're headed. The ride can be very uncomfortable and if you are lucky enough to reach your destination, you do so feeling confused, anxious, stressed, and worn down.

Which road do you want to be on? Now, answer the next question honestly.

Which road are you on right now?

I feel so many people are in survival mode because at some point along their journey they were on the confident road when they experienced their Identity Crisis. As a result, they took a wrong turn and got lost. Maybe someone gave them bad directions or ran them off the road. Either way, they feel stuck, confused, anxious, stressed, and worn down. They forgot what confidence felt like and became insecure.

Three years ago I scheduled a meeting with my CEO because I wanted to talk to him about hiring an Executive Coach. When he asked me why, I told him I wanted unshakable confidence and that I recognize in some situations I'm not as confident as I want to be. I was committed to reaching my goals.

His response:

"Jason, here's the deal. Right now you're on a boat. Your sail is up, the wind is strong, and it's blowing in the direction you want it to. Focus on sailing your boat. Sometimes you are so busy looking for little rips in your sail or trying to add to it, that you aren't focused on sailing your boat. Your boat is good. Its sail is good. The wind is blowing. Stop looking for problems to fix and sail your boat."

That simple analogy helped me become more confident and it changed the way I saw my insecurities. Soon after, when I felt insecurity creeping up, I asked myself if it was a legitimate problem that needed my attention or just a tiny rip. Ninety percent of the time they are tiny rips. I was focused on confidently sailing my boat.

If you only take away one thing from this book, I would like it to be this section. Confidence and insecurity are key factors in living the life you deserve. We need to understand how important confidence is and why it is critical to protect it. We also need to understand that if we fail to manage our insecurities, they can hold us down and keep us down forever.

On the next page, circle the words that you can relate to most.

Confident	Insecure
Bold	Uncertain
Convinced	Worried
Courageous	Afraid
Fearless	Anxious
Hopeful	Apprehensive
Positive	Cowardly
Satisfied	Depressed
Self-assured	Doubtful
Self-reliant	Hesitant
Sure	Pessimistic
Upbeat	Sad
Brave	Touchy
Secure	Troubled
Self-Sufficient	Unsure
Trusting	Uptight
Unafraid	Jealous
At Ease	On thin ice
Calm	Questioning
Collected	Touch and go
Certain	Unassured
Composed	Unconfident
Safe	Weak

People who are confident feel the descriptors on the left. People who are insecure feel the descriptors on the right.

Protecting Your Confidence.

In order to be confident and maintain confidence, we need to understand it first. We must also understand insecurities so we can manage them as we feel them, because they are manageable.

I was a very insecure kid growing up; there were many emotions in the insecure list that resonated with me. I wasn't confident in anything I did whether it was academics, sports, or social situations. I think I had a lot of friends and productive relationships, but I always felt anxious, and I was a follower.

The farther I come along on this personal, professional, and leadership development journey, and the more I have learned about the world, the more I have learned about confidence and insecurity. The more I've understood them, the better I've been able to manage it within my own life. Insecurity management is a game changer.

In 2009 and 2010, I served as VP of Professional Development for the Young Professional Connection (YPC) in Des Moines. I joined YPC in July of 2008, and I attended my first professional development committee meeting. The meeting was scheduled to start at 6 P.M. and I walked in around 5:55 P.M.. I remember walking in and seeing a group of well-dressed young professionals sitting around tables talking. I got nervous and walked by them, hoping that wasn't the meeting I was looking for. After walking around the restaurant and bar area once, I realized that was the meeting I was supposed to attend. I got anxious, intimidated, and scared and I walked right by them and out the door, but that made me uncomfortable as well. I was insecure and it was easier for me to avoid the discomfort than work through it. I stopped in the parking lot and said to myself, "Jason, what the hell are you worried about? Get back in there." So, I turned around and walked back in. I cautiously approached the group and asked if they were the YPC and they said they were. And, you know what? They were awesome. So awesome, in fact, that four months later I was VP of that committee.

That was a defining moment for me, and today I'm pretty good about knowing when something is off and I'm not as confident as I need to be. I have learned over the years that my potential for insecurity is the greatest when I don't get enough sleep or I'm not exercising on a regular basis. When I do feel insecure I try to resolve the issue.

Insecurity will control us if we let it. Being on the insecure road is like a disease that slowly eats at us until we are paralyzed. Insecurity kills our relationships, self-esteem, and potential. We have to protect our confidence and manage our insecurities.

CHAPTER 5

A Framework for Your Confident Life

Six months after I made the commitment to learn about success, I wrote a paper for my Psychology of Success class on the topic of motivation. I wanted to know why people do the things they do. When I started my research, I came across Abraham Maslow and his 1943 Psychology Review article titled "A Theory of Human Motivation," where he outlines Maslow's Hierarchy of Needs. I started reading it one Saturday night while visiting my mom. I remember having plans to go partying with buddies, but ended up ditching them to finish reading. I was hooked! I didn't understand everything I was reading, but that didn't matter; I couldn't put it down. Fourteen-years later Maslow's Hierarchy of Needs continues to be a foundation for how I approach my life and work with others.

Maslow's Hierarchy of Needs

Maslow's Hierarchy of Needs is a theory that says human beings have five levels of needs:

1. Physiological / Survival
   (air, water, food, sleep, sex)

2. Safety / Security
   (physical and emotional safety & security)

3. Social / Love
   (belonging, friendship, love, sexual intimacy)

4. Esteem / Achievement
   (self-esteem, confidence, respect)

5. Self-Actualization
   (purpose, creativity, peace, potential)

The way this theory works is that until our lowest level (physiological) needs are met, we won't naturally be motivated to satisfy our higher level needs. For example, some physiological needs are air to breathe, water to drink, food to eat, and sleep. The theory suggests that if those needs aren't met, we won't be as motivated (if motivated at all) to satisfy our need for safety and security, social and love, esteem and achievement, or self-actualization and purpose.[6]

If you are starving and your nutrients are depleted, that will be your focus. You won't be able to control it; your body will crave it. You will have little to no concern about your need for safety, love, esteem, or self-actualization. Think about what happens to you when you don't get enough sleep. When you are grouchy are you focused on social needs and love? Do you feel like achieving more? Are you concerned with your purpose? No, you're tired and want to get some rest.

The second need for safety and security is where I want to focus our attention. This need covers everything from the need of physical safety from danger to emotional security. Everything we are talking about in this section is about confidence versus emotional insecurity.

Maslow's theory suggests that if your need for safety and security is not met–in other words, you are on the insecure road–your focus will be on satisfying your need for security with little or no focus on your higher level needs of social, love, esteem, achievement, or self-actualization.

My Professional Development Committee meeting with the YPC is a great example of this. I almost skipped that meeting because I was nervous and scared. Walking out made me feel safe and secure. In that moment, I wasn't focused on making new friends (social / love). I wasn't thinking about how it would help me achieve success (esteem / achievement). I wasn't living my purpose (self-actualization). The fear and insecurity motivated me to walk out. Thankfully, I caught myself, recognized my insecurity, and walked back in. According to Maslow, insecurity may prevent you from:

- Building and maintaining healthy relationships (Social / Love)

- Having self-esteem to achieve all you are capable of (Esteem / Achievement)

- Discovering your passions and living your purpose. (Self-Actualization)

Why is this important?

1. You must understand insecurities and how paralyzing they can be.

2. You must understand your insecurities so you can manage them.

3. You must manage your insecurities so you can live
   a confident life.

What insecurities are preventing you from living a confident
life?

_____

_____

_____

_____

_____

_____

_____

_____

_____

_____

_____

Introduction to the Eight Key Areas

I want to introduce you to a way of looking at your life
that will give you greater awareness, balance, control, and
confidence. If we are not intentional, life can feel like a
messy desk where random piles of papers are scattered all
over the place. You may have an idea which pile has your
important papers, but you're not sure what to do with everything else. What do you throw away and what do you keep?
At some point you realize you need an organization system
and a trash can.

The eight key areas will help you organize your life so you know what needs your attention now, what can be filed away for later, and what needs to be tossed in the trash. They will help you focus on the right things, for the right reasons.

Picture your world in the eight key areas:

1. Values, Standards, and Passions

2. Home Culture

3. Health

4. Finances

5. Relationships

6. Career

7. Fun

8. Impact

I don't believe there is a stress or insecurity we deal with that doesn't come from our Home, Health, Finances, Relationships, and/or Career. Think about everything that stresses you out. I bet the cause is in one of those areas. As adults we are responsible for balancing and managing each of these areas. Lack of balance and fulfillment in these areas will lead to stress and insecurity.

Take a moment to observe the world around you. People all around us are dominated by insecurity; struggling to feel successful, find meaning, and create balance in one or more of the key areas of life. You might be saying to yourself, "That will never happen to me," and I hope you are right. But insecurities impact people who have goals, aspirations, and dreams. They impact people who were likely fired up about the world in their early and mid-20s. Life has a funny way of kicking you in the ass if you aren't paying attention to the right things. The better we know our values, standards, and passions, and the more we are able to align our actions within each area, the more confidence and fulfillment we will experience. Finally, the more fulfillment we experience in these eight areas, the more we will be in a position to impact the world around us.

Before we move too far along with this model, it's important that we are able to look at these eight areas from two different perspectives.

Perspective #1

Each area is important and needs your individual attention.

Whether we have clearly articulated them or not, we have expectations for ourselves in each of the eight areas. If we don't see them as individual areas that are equally important, they could get lost in the mix, leading to stress and insecurity.

Additionally, we want to be able to identify when a specific area is the source of stress and insecurity so we can address root causes rather than basing them on confusion and random feelings. A really important example of this is relationships. A woman doesn't feel good because she is insecure with her body, but doesn't realize it. All she knows is that she is not happy and it starts to impact her relationships. All of a sudden, because she can't find happiness, she starts to question her relationship thinking it may be her partner. Her partner doesn't make her happy. Her insecurity within was the root cause of the stress, not her partner.

Perspective #2

Though each area is important and needs your individual attention, they are all connected and impact each other.

Focusing on one area will impact the other areas. Let's

say you are going to focus on your health and you buy supplements, hire a personal trainer, and commit more time to achieving your health goals.

- How does this new focus impact your financial goals?
- How does your new time commitment impact the people around you?

Here's another example: your new job pays more and is good for your finances. How do the longer hours impact your health and relationships?

When you recognize that everything is connected and you know what your expectations are in each critical area of your life, your decisions will be more responsible and meaningful. How do you make decisions today? Maybe you are spontaneous and make quick decisions. Perhaps you know what you want and you go after it. Maybe you do research and analyze. Perhaps you seek guidance from your family or friends. When I was between the ages of 18 and 23, I probably didn't have a concrete answer. In fact, I know people in their 30's that can't answer the question. Because of the magnitude of the question, it's important that you have an answer.

Confidence in the eight key areas will continue to be a theme throughout the rest of this book. It's a simple but effective concept that will allow you to organize your world, move forward with confidence, and focus on the right things for the right reasons.

CHAPTER 6

Values, Standards, & Passions

Values = What is important to you?

Standards = What are your expectations?

Passions = What excites you?

While I was trying to figure out my values, standards, and passions, I called my mother. A few years prior, she was fortunate enough to retire from the manufacturing area of an aviation company she worked with for close to 30 years. I always assumed the pay was fair and it gave our family security and stability, but I know she didn't love it.

When I called her, I asked her one question; I asked her if she could change one thing about her life, what would it be? She said "I would have stayed in school to become a preschool or kindergarten teacher." Deep down I knew that, but it was hard to hear her say it. She would have loved being a preschool or kindergarten teacher. She loves little kids and is amazing with them. In her early 20's, she quit college and never went back. She spent the next 30 years married to an abusive alcoholic and going to a job she didn't love. Man, it broke my heart, but it also lit a fire within me.

After hearing that from my mother, I made the commitment to myself that I was not going to allow that to happen to me and that I was going to do what I needed to do to live the life I wanted to live. It started with reconnecting to my values, standards, and passions.

> *"When your values are clear to you, making decisions becomes easier."* - *Roy Disney*

Over the next few pages you are going to be asked to think about your world in the present and the future and articulate your thoughts. These might feel like big questions if you've never thought about them before, but I promise you, there is a method behind the madness. Just be honest with yourself and do your best.

Where are you now?

On a scale of 1–10, rate your happiness in the following areas of your life.

Home Culture: _____

Health: _____

Finances: _____

Relationships: _____

Career: _____

Fun: _____

Impact: _____

How balanced and fulfilled are you?

What does a 10 look like in each area?

Take a moment to dream a bit. In a few sentences, describe what a perfect 10 looks like in each area.

Home Culture:

Health:

Finances:

Relationships:

Career:

Fun:

Impact:

Drilling Down

When you think about what a 10 looks like in each area, in the spaces on the following pages, articulate five things you **DON'T WANT** in each area, as well things you **DO WANT** in each area.

In the DON'T WANT column, really think about things you don't want in each area.

For example, in my Home, I don't want people yelling, my house to be a mess, or for it to be cluttered with too many things. With my Health, I don't want to be overweight, sick, or stressed. With my Finances, I don't want high debt, poor credit, or little savings. With my relationships, I don't want to be distant from my mother and sister, fight with my significant other, or fail to spend enough quality time with my children.

What don't you want in your life?

In the DO WANT column, write five things you DO WANT.

For example, with my Career, I want to be passionate, rewarded financially, and make a difference in people's lives. With Fun, I want to have freedom, get out of my comfort zone, and see new places. With Impact, I want to make a difference in people's lives and donate time and money to worthy causes.

In the spaces below and on the following page, please complete what you DON'T WANT and what you DO WANT in each area of your life.

HOME CULTURE	
I Don't Want	I Do Want

HEALTH	
I Don't Want	**I Do Want**

FINANCES	
I Don't Want	**I Do Want**

RELATIONSHIPS

I Don't Want	I Do Want

CAREER

I Don't Want	I Do Want

FUN	
I Don't Want	**I Do Want**

IMPACT	
I Don't Want	**I Do Want**

Nice work!

As you were filling in your DON'T WANTS and DO WANTS, I hope you realized the desires you have in each area. I hope you realized the things you must avoid if you want to achieve everything you want. Everyone talks about what they want, but few think about what they need to avoid to get it.

Who Do You Know?

Now that you've taken some time to articulate and understand what you DON'T and DO WANT in each area of your life, think of someone that has what you want in each area; this could be a family member, friend, someone in your professional network you admire, or someone you don't personally know but admire.

If you are having trouble coming up with your own words to describe the people who have what you want, reference the list of values on page 52.

Who has the HOME CULTURE you want?				
What five words would you use to describe them?				

Who has the HEALTHY lifestyle you would like?

What five words would you use to describe them?

Who is in the FINANCIAL situation you want to be in?

What five words would you use to describe them?

Who has the types of RELATIONSHIPS you desire to have?

What five words would you use to describe them?

Who has the fulfillment in their CAREER you want to have?

What five words would you use to describe them?

Who has the level of FUN that you desire?

What five words would you use to describe them?

Who is making the kind of IMPACT you want to make?

What five words would you use to describe them?

Good work!

If you completed the exercise on the previous pages, you wrote down a total of 35 values to describe the people who, in some capacity, have the life you desire.

adaptable	exuberant	pioneering
adventurous	fair-minded	philosophical
affable	faithful	placid
affectionate	fearless	plucky
agreeable	forceful	polite
ambitious	frank	powerful
amiable	friendly	practical
amicable	funny	pro-active
amusing	generous	quick-witted
brave	gentle	quiet
bright	good	rational
broad-minded	gregarious	reliable
calm	hard-working	reserved
careful	helpful	resourceful
charming	honest	romantic
communicative	humorous	self-confident
compassionate	imaginative	self-disciplined
conscientious	impartial	sensible
considerate	independent	sensitive
convivial	intellectual	shy
courageous	intelligent	sincere
courteous	intuitive	sociable
creative	inventive	straightforward
decisive	kind	sympathetic
determined	loving	thoughtful
diligent	loyal	tidy
diplomatic	modest	tough
discreet	neat	unassuming
dynamic	nice	understanding
easygoing	optimistic	versatile
emotional	passionate	warmhearted
energetic	patient	willing
enthusiastic	persistent	witty

CHAPTER 7

Bringing It All Together

Let's bring it all together!

Over the past few pages you have:

- Rated your happiness in seven key areas of your life

- Defined what a perfect 10 looks like in each key area

- Acknowledged things you DON'T want and DO want in your life

- Described people who live the kind of life you desire

Take a moment to review everything you have done.

On pages 49-51 you wrote down 35 different values to describe people who live the life you desire to live. On page 52, there are a total of 99 different values outlined for your reference.

As you look at all those values, think about what type of person you need to be to get what you want out of life and leave the legacy you outlined. How do you need to show up every single day?

Using the list of values from pages 49-52, write down the 10 values you feel you must live if you are going get what you want and live the life you desire:

1._____   6. _____

2._____   7. _____

3._____   8. _____

4._____   9. _____

5._____   10. _____

Out of the 10 values you identified as important, which 5 are most critical to you to accomplish everything you want in your life? Why are they critical?

5 Critical Values	Why are they critical to your success?
1.	
2.	
3.	
4.	
5.	

Your Focus Statement

Create your Focus Statement using the five values that are critical to you being the person you need to be to live the life you desire.

1st Draft

I will succeed because I will focus on . . .

_____

_____

_____

_____

_____

_____

For many of you, this is the first time you have ever been challenged to think about these questions. There is no right or wrong way to do this. The only requirement I have is that whatever you come up with excites you and reminds you of the type of person you need to be to live the life you want to live.

Here is an example of my five critical values and my Focus Statement:

    i. Confident
    ii. Authentic
    iii. Considerate
    iv. Passionate
    v. Inspiring

My Focus Statement:

I will succeed because I will focus on living with confidence and authenticity. I will be considerate toward others, passionate about the world, and inspire others to confidently pursue and achieve meaningful results.

Use the spaces below to practice writing versions of your Focus Statement. Use the one that provokes excitement and inspires you the most.

I will succeed because I will focus on . . .

_____

_____

_____

_____

_____

_____

I will succeed because I will focus on . . .

_____

_____

_____

_____

_____

_____

I will succeed because I will focus on . . .

_____

_____

_____

_____

_____

_____

I will succeed because I will focus on . . .

_____

_____

_____

_____

_____

_____

I will succeed because I will focus on . . .

_____

_____

_____

_____

_____

Your five critical values and your Focus Statement will serve as your guide as we move forward in creating your vision, setting your goals, and creating your plan.

Please write your five critical values for the center your model below.

1. _____

2. _____

3. _____

4. _____

5. _____

I understand this might feel kind of heavy, but this approach will change your life. Successful people get this. What they already know is that to live the life you desire, your life must be a reflection of your values, standards, and passions. Those three factors must be the center of our decision making and how we live our lives. If we make decisions based on our values, standards, and passions, everything we experience will be more meaningful and fulfilling.

CHAPTER 8

Putting the Vision into Place

Millenials and people in their 20's get a bad rap for lacking motivation. If you take this seriously and allow your values to guide your life, you are going to separate yourself from the stereotype others your age have created. I used to leverage this track in my mid-20's. I knew if I could get in front of the right person, I would impress them with my self-awareness and self-management. Young adults your age don't talk about this and unfortunately, many of them won't ever learn it. This is your opportunity to learn and live what the most successful people in the world know.

In the previous section you defined what a perfect 10 in happiness was in each area of your life. You thought about what you DON'T and DO want. With your five critical values, you acknowledged the person you need to be to have the life you want to have. It's time to put everything into your vision.

Please take a moment and think about your life five years from now. What do you want it to look like?

- What do you want your Home Culture to be?

- What kind of Health will you be in?

- What will your Finances look like?

- How healthy will your Relationships be?

- What are you doing in your Career?

- How much Fun are you having?

- How are you Impacting the world around you?

I created my first vision when I was 24. When I created it, I called it my "By 30 Vision," with the intention that I was going to accomplish my vision by the time I turned 30. Now you might recall part of my vision was to be a coach, counselor, teacher, trainer, or speaker. I had an Associate's degree and knew I needed at minimum of a Bachelor's degree, or maybe even a Master's degree. I picked my 30th birthday, as I felt that would give me enough time to get my educational and professional experiences in order.

As you are creating your vision, you may realize that five years is too long or too little. Adjust your timeframe as needed. What you don't want to do is set unrealistic expectations for yourself. So many people never reach their goals because they don't set realistic expectations. What is important is that you're imagining a meaningful life that is based on your values and passions and you are writing your vision down.

The next time I recreated my vision, I was probably 30 or 31 years old. At the time I was a Business Coach, and I knew in the future I wanted to travel around the country facilitating coaching and training with leaders. I created a vision board, which was a visual representation of my dream. In the center was a guy with blond hair, wearing a suit, standing in front of a boardroom table, with a view of skyscrapers outside of the windows.

Today, I travel across the United States facilitating leadership training for clients.

I'm evidence that there is something to solidifying your vision. It allows you to dream of what is possible in the world, but it requires you to focus on what you really want in your life. Over the next several pages, you are going to create your five-year vision for each area of your life. This is your chance to dream and fantasize about what the world can look like for you in five years.

As you are writing your vision, write as if it is happening right now. For example, rather than saying, "I want to lose 20 pounds and get to a weight of 210," I will say, "I've lost 20 pounds and currently weigh 210 pounds, and I feel awesome!"

Don't overthink this. There are no right or wrong answers.

"In order to carry a positive action we must develop here a positive vision."
– Dalai Lama

Good luck!

What does your HOME CULTURE look like in five years?

_____

_____

_____

_____

_____

_____

_____

_____

_____

_____

_____

_____

_____

_____

_____

_____

_____

_____

_____

_____

_____

_____

_____

_____

_____

_____

_____

_____

What is your HEALTH like in five years?

_____

_____

_____

_____

_____

_____

_____

_____

_____

_____

_____

_____

_____

_____

_____

_____

_____

_____

_____

_____

_____

_____

_____

What are your FINANCES like in five years?

_____

_____

_____

_____

_____

_____

_____

_____

_____

_____

_____

_____

_____

_____

_____

_____

_____

_____

_____

_____

_____

What types of RELATIONSHIPS do you have five years?

_____

_____

_____

_____

_____

_____

_____

_____

_____

_____

_____

_____

_____

_____

_____

_____

_____

_____

_____

_____

_____

What does your CAREER look like in five years?

_____

_____

_____

_____

_____

_____

_____

_____

_____

_____

_____

_____

_____

_____

_____

_____

_____

_____

_____

How do you have FUN in five years?

_____

_____

_____

_____

_____

_____

_____

_____

_____

_____

_____

_____

_____

_____

_____

_____

_____

_____

_____

_____

_____

_____

_____

_____

What IMPACT do you have in five years?

_____

_____

_____

_____

_____

_____

_____

_____

_____

_____

_____

_____

_____

_____

_____

_____

_____

_____

_____

_____

_____

_____

_____

_____

Congratulations on completing your visions for the key areas. Together these smaller visions create the bigger vision for your life. If you hand-wrote your visions on the provided pages, take a moment to type them into a single document.

CHAPTER 9

Fulfilling Your Vision with SMART Goals

Next, I would like you to get a highlighter. Review your vision for each of the seven areas and highlight the goals you want to accomplish within each vision.

For example, in my health area, my vision may say:

> I keep my mind sharp by reading and learning every single day about things I am passionate about. When I'm facing emotional challenges, I don't bottle them up and seek help and advice from a trusted friend, mentor, or advisor.

> I am the healthiest I've ever been. I weigh 210 pounds and make it to the gym at least six days per week. I am eating better than I have ever eaten, with my nutrients around 30% protein, 45% carbohydrates, and 25% fats per day. I love the way I feel, and I never run out of energy playing with my children. Sleep is very important to my health so I make sure I get at least seven hours of sleep every night. To ensure I stay as healthy as I can, I get annual physicals and go to my physician as soon as I start feeling ill. Over the past two

years I have accomplished a few activity goals as well. I completed a Tough Mudder and my first half marathon.

Just in this short excerpt I can identify a number of things I would like to accomplish:

- Read and learn every day
- Seek advice when facing emotional challenges
- I want to weigh 210 pounds
- I want to go to the gym six days per week
- I want my nutritional intake to be balanced
- I want to sleep seven hours per night
- I will get annual physicals
- I will go to the doctor when I am sick
- I will complete a Tough Mudder
- I will complete a half marathon

Everything listed are actions I want to take to make my health a perfect 10 rating. I know if I am able to accomplish the goals listed I will be mentally, emotionally, and physically healthy.

Use the following pages to write down the goals you have highlighted for each area of your life.

My HOME CULTURE Goals are:

1.
2.
3.
4.
5.
6.
7.
8.
9.
10.

My HEALTH Goals are:

1.
2.
3.
4.
5.
6.
7.
8.
9.
10.

My FINANCIAL Goals are:

1.
2.
3.
4.
5.
6.
7.
8.
9.
10.

My RELATIONSHIP Goals are:

1.
2.
3.
4.
5.
6.
7.
8.
9.
10.

My CAREER Goals are:

1.
2.
3.
4.
5.
6.
7.
8.
9.
10.

My FUN Goals are:

1.
2.
3.
4.
5.
6.
7.
8.
9.
10.

My IMPACT Goals are:
1.
2.
3.
4.
5.
6.
7.
8.
9.
10.

A few notes about goals.

Your goals should meet five pieces of criteria. They should be specific, measurable, attainable, relevant, and time bound; otherwise known as **SMART GOALS**.[7]

SPECIFIC – What do you want to accomplish?

MEASURABLE – How will you measure your success?

ATTAINABLE – What makes it possible?

RELEVANT – Why is this important?

TIME BOUND – By what date will you achieve your goal?

As an example I will SMART Goal one of my goals:

SPECIFIC - I want to weigh 210 pounds.

MEASURABLE - I will lose between one and two pounds per week and I will weigh myself on a weekly basis.

ATTAINABLE - This is attainable because I will align my eating and exercise habits with my goal of weighing 210 pounds.

RELEVANT – Weighing 210 pounds will be the result of a healthy lifestyle consistent with my values.

TIME BOUND - If I lose one pound per week it will take me 12 weeks to weigh 210 pounds. I will weigh 210 pounds by October 1st.

"I want to weigh 210 pounds. I will lose one pound per week by aligning my eating and exercise habits with my goal. I will weigh 210 pounds by October 1st and will weigh myself on a weekly basis to ensure I'm on track. Weighing 210 pounds aligns with my health values and the healthy man I want to be."

Write Your Broad Goal (I want to):
SMART Goal it:
SPECIFIC - What do you want to accomplish?
MEASURABLE - How will you measure your success?
ATTAINABLE - What makes it possible?
RELEVANT - Why is this important?
TIME BOUND - By what date will your achieve your goal?

Write Your SMART Goal:

_____

_____

_____

_____

_____

By now you're either feeling really excited or a little overwhelmed. Nice work, if you've made it this far. Most people think only about what they want right now, and very few think about what they want in the future. If you don't know what you want, how are you supposed to get it?

This is about knowing who you are, what you want, and going after it thoughtfully and responsibly. You don't want to be that person who wakes up one day regretting the past. You don't want to be that person who gets excited and makes an impulsive decision that hurts yourself or other people.

When you create a vision, set goals, and make decisions based on what is important to you (values) and things that excite you about the world (passion), your journey to achieve your goals and fulfill your vision will be meaningful. It's the ultimate motivation you need to take your life to the next level!

Now, let's figure out how you're going to do it!

CHAPTER 10

Creating Your Plan

Your whole life you have been following somebody else's plan. Your parents, teachers, and coaches all had a plan for you. If you went to college, you had schedules and syllabi to follow if you wanted to be successful. If you are working full time, hopefully your employer has provided you with a plan or roadmap for success.

This is your opportunity to create *your* plan. This is your chance to figure out what it is going to take to get the life you desire. Successful people don't obtain success by accident. First, they make the decision that they want it, and they have an understanding of what it will take to achieve it. Second, they have a plan to achieve it. This is the plan that will guarantee meaningful results in your life; results that you, your parents, grandparents, and everyone who cares about you will be proud of.

Take a moment to revisit the goals you outlined in the last section. If you still have the highlighter handy, go ahead and highlight the goals that are most meaningful to you. Now, it's time to create your action plan. Your action plan will have a few sections as bulleted below:

- Result – What result do you want to achieve?

- Success Steps – What steps need to be taken to achieve the desired result?

- Resources – What resources will you need to successfully complete the Success Steps in pursuit of achieving your desired results?

    - Will you need time to complete certain steps?

    - Will you need to spend money to achieve your result?

    - Who do you know that can help you?

    - Who do you need to connect with?

    - Will you need special technology to achieve your results?

    - What do you need to learn to achieve your results?

    - What else?

- Deadline – When will you achieve the desired result?

- Measurement – How will you measure it to ensure you are on track?

The purpose of the template on the following pages is to get you to start thinking about the process and plan to achieve your goals and vision. Nothing is set in stone and can be changed anytime you wish.

At minimum, the template is all about building awareness about the steps you need to take to achieve your goals and fulfill your vision. Some of you will enjoy the level of detail these templates allow you to get into.

Either way this is about:

- Knowing what is important to you (values)
- Knowing what excites you (passions)
- Creating a vision that aligns with your values and passions
- Understanding what you need to accomplish to fulfill your vision
- Knowing the direction you want to go and what steps you need to take

What result do you want to achieve?

What steps do you need to take to achieve your desired results?

What resources will you need?

TIME	MONEY	PEOPLE
TECHNOLOGY	INFORMATION	OTHER SUPPLIES

When will you achieve your desired result?

How will you measure your progress?

What could prevent you from achieving it?

Can you think of anything else?

"If you don't design your own life plan, chances are you'll fall into someone else's plan. And guess what they have planned for you? Not much." – Jim Rohn

CHAPTER 11

Working Your Plan

This is where the rubber meets the road. Up to now you've done a lot of thinking. It's time to put those thoughts into action. Because your plan was created from your values and passions, taking action on your plan should be easy. Every action you take will be meaningful, even the steps that are more challenging and not very fun.

The only way I was going to achieve my "By 30 Vision" was to complete my undergraduate degree. I finished my AAS when I was 21, took a few classes when I was 24, but didn't really start to seriously complete my undergraduate degree until I was 27. I had responsibilities like rent, car payments, insurance, and child support. I had to work full-time while I was in school. I had class for four hours every Wednesday night and every other night was filled with tons of reading and writing papers. Most of the time it wasn't fun, but I never thought about quitting. I knew what was important to me and what excited me. I knew my vision and what I needed to do to fulfill my vision. Quitting was never an option. During my first year back in school I even had my manager have a serious talk with me, where he pressured me to quit or postpone school so I could focus more time and energy at work. I didn't even have to think about my answer.

NOPE! That job wasn't going to fulfill my vision–only my education would. End of conversation.

The journey in achieving your vision may not always be fun or easy, but neither is spending the rest of your life in uncertainty, confusion, and insecurity. We owe it to ourselves to take action to get what we want.

Double Vision

When people set goals, create plans, and take action, they tend to focus on a pain point or a specific need. The reason we organized your visions in the critical areas of your life is so you could start off by seeing the big picture. I often talk to clients about the need to have "Double Vision." Double Vision is your ability to give laser focus to a specific goal you are trying to accomplish, while also having the ability to see how your focus and pursuit on one area impacts other important areas and goals.

You are not doing yourself or your vision any good if you are rocking and rolling in one area of your life, but you are crashing and burning in other areas. Double Vision allows you to maintain balance and control while achieving your goals.[8]

Dealing with the Doubters

By now, you've probably heard the phrase "Haters gonna hate," and, they will! When you start working your plan you might scare some people who are close to you. You are going to have people close to you who won't understand what you are trying to do. They won't respect your values and passions and they will tell you all day long how and why you are doing it wrong. I had friends tell me I was crazy for going back and spending time and money in school. I had one who regularly said, "Kiesau, you could be making $100,000 per year right now doing sales. Why are you spending more money on school?" He didn't understand or respect what I was trying to accomplish. It wasn't about money; it was about meaning. It was about doing what I wanted to do and living the life I wanted to live.

My family was no different. I had a family member make snide comments about what I was trying to accomplish. I had to lovingly ignore them and dismiss what they were saying. They didn't care to understand. Now, I'm not telling you to dismiss everyone who doesn't see things the way you do; that is not productive. But you are going to come across people who simply don't get it, and worse, they don't respect it. Part of this journey is knowing what information and people to pay attention to and what information and people to ignore. You will not please everyone so you need not try. You'll drive yourself crazy and risk ending up on the insecure road.

What I learned is that most people didn't support me because they didn't understand what I was trying to accomplish. The first thing I had to do was reassure them that I knew what I was doing. It didn't take long before people started to get it. Even my harshest critics became supportive and the more consistent I was, the more they supported, trusted, and respected my decisions.

Create Momentum and Quiet Doubters by Taking Consistent Action

Taking action on your plan will accomplish two goals.

i. It will create momentum. The more things you do that are meaningful, the more motivated you will be to continue. As you cross off your steps to success, the better you will feel and the more confident you will become. It won't be long before you will have so much momentum created that you will feel unstoppable.

ii. The more action you take and the more momentum you create, the more you will quiet any doubters or haters like the ones I previously mentioned. People cannot argue with results, and as you get results you'll earn their respect in the process. Let's assume your family and friends want the best for you, but change scares everyone. In both cases I spoke about, at some point they backed off and appreciated what I was trying to accomplish. Consistent action in the right direction will always prevail!

CHAPTER 12

Making an Impact

I remember when I was 21 and finished my associate's degree. I felt unstoppable and couldn't wait to blaze my trail. I also remember being very "me-focused" and selfish. I was worried about my path and my future. My mom and I frequently argued because I thought I had everything figured out. I remember judging people around me that I didn't agree with. Though I am a relationship-oriented person, I was "me-focused" rather than "we-focused." To a certain extent, I think that is perfectly normal, but just because it's normal doesn't mean it's right or productive.

One of the most valuable lessons I learned during my Identity Crisis was the concept of the win-win, which happens to be habit number four in Stephen Covey's *The 7 Habits of Highly Effective People*. Win-Win means regardless of the situation you are in, everyone comes out a winner. In order for this to happen, all parties involved need to be bold enough to ask for what they want, and at the same time be willing to listen and accommodate others. The win-win is about you and everyone else involved feeling good about what is going on. The win-win means you are approaching all situations with your eyes and ears open so you understand what other people value and help them come out a winner as well. This isn't about putting other people's needs ahead of your own. That would be a lose-win. It's about everyone getting what they need.[9]

It's Not About You

The more you learn about the world, the more you will understand that it's not about you. It's not about what you have achieved, a position you hold, or power you think you have. It's about people. It's about the people you come in contact with every single day, and I'm talking about anyone: your partner, coworkers, or the lady checking you out at the gas station on the corner. It's about how you communicate with them and make them feel. It's about the impression you leave with them.

When you start living life according to your values and passions, people will notice. They will notice your focus, confidence, and spirit. The more consistent you are, the more trust you will build. You will stand out because the average person doesn't show up like this, and you'll have the ability to make a greater impact on those around you.

Maximize Your Impact

Take a moment to think about all the roles you play in your life. Consider the roles you wish to play in the future.

For example, I am a

- Son
- Brother

- Father
- Partner
- Uncle
- Grandson
- Nephew
- Cousin
- Friend
- Coworker
- Employee
- Mentor
- Student
- Business Partner
- Board Member

Think about the five most important roles that you play in your life.

What are they?

_____

_____

_____

_____

_____

_____

_____

_____

_____

_____

When you think about each of the five roles, consider what kind of person you need to be and the impact you want to have on the people who depend on you.

Use the spaces on the next couple of pages to articulate your thoughts further.

Role #1

What kind of person do you want to be?

What kind of impact do you want to have?

Role #2

What kind of person do you want to be?

What kind of impact do you want to have?

Role #3

What kind of person do you want to be?

What kind of impact do you want to have?

Role #4

What kind of person do you want to be?

What kind of impact do you want to have?

Role #5

What kind of person do you want to be?

What kind of impact do you want to have?

It doesn't matter what age you are; we all have the ability to make the world a better place. We have the ability to change things for the better, to impact people's lives positively. We have the ability to inspire others and make a difference.

Are You a Lantern or a Lamp?

The greatest freedom we have–and the one many people give up–is the freedom of choice. You have the freedom to choose who you want to be and how you want to impact the world. Whether or not you intentionally exercise that freedom of choice, you impact the world around you.

What is your impact?

Is it positive? Do you leave things better than when you found them? Do you even care?

An analogy I like to use is **The Lamp & Lantern**.

Let's start with the lamp.

Lamps are valuable as they shine light wherever they stand. Lamps help people see clearer and allow them to maneuver in the darkest places. However, a lamp's impact is limited. They stay in one position, and therefore only shine light in one place. You have to come to the lamp, and they are only valuable if you are beneath them.

How about the lantern?

Though they serve the same purpose, the lantern's opportunity to impact is much greater, which makes it more valuable.

For starters, the lantern is mobile. Wherever it goes, its

light benefits everyone around it. It isn't designed to stand above people or stay in one place. It will go wherever light is needed. It can be hung high or sit low, which gives it the ability to provide light from different perspectives. It's designed to go beside you. Its handle is its offer to help; just grab it!

Are you more like the lamp or the lantern?

Do you stay in one place and only shine your light on those who stand beneath you? Or does your light shine everywhere you go, impacting everyone around you?

I like the lantern.

The unfortunate reality is many people aren't even aware they possess this light and have no clue of their potential to positively impact people and the world around them. Maybe it's with their spirit or attitude or passion. For some reason, people don't allow this light to shine.

What if you were a lantern and allowed your spirit, attitude, and passion to confidently shine on everyone around you? Think about the impact you would have on them.

> *"Before you are a leader, success is all about growing yourself. When you become a leader, success is all about growing others."*
> – Jack Welch

CHAPTER 13

Leaving a Legacy

A couple of years ago a friend of mine asked me what I wanted written on my gravestone. It turned out to be one of the most powerful questions I have been asked. At first I tried to stay high-level and wanted it to say "Jason made the world a better place." Though I liked it, being a dad is very meaningful to me, and I thought it should mention something about my children. I wasn't satisfied with that either, because I don't solely want to be remembered as a great dad, I want to be remembered as a great family man and a great man all around.

How do you want to be remembered?

I want you to think about your funeral years and years down the road. At your funeral, four different people are going to stand up and say a few words about you. The four people are:

- A close family member

- A close friend

- A co-worker

- A neighbor or someone you knew outside of work

Each of them is going to talk about four things:

    i.   What kind of attitude you had.

    ii. How you personally made them feel.

    iii. Your greatest accomplishment.

    iv. The impact you had on the world around you.

What do you hope they will say about you? Please complete the worksheet on the following pages:

At your funeral, what does your CLOSE FAMILY MEMBER say about...
Your attitude:
How you made them feel:
Your greatest accomplishment:
The impact you had on the world around you:

At your funeral, what does your CLOSE FRIEND say about...

Your attitude:

How you made them feel:

Your greatest accomplishment:

The impact you had on the world around you:

At your funeral, what does your CO-WORKER say about...

Your attitude:

How you made them feel:

Your greatest accomplishment:

The impact you had on the world around you:

At your funeral, what does your NEIGHBOR say about...

Your attitude:
How you made them feel:
Your greatest accomplishment:
The impact you had on the world around you:

What legacy did you leave?

In one sentence, write what you would like your gravestone to say:

_____

_____

_____

_____

_____

_____

_____

_____

_____

_____

CHAPTER 14

A Whole New World

I was 23 when I started learning about value-based decision-making and taking consistent action on my vision. As soon as my decisions became a reflection of my values and passions, the world started changing. I was more focused than I had ever been. I felt more productive and confident than I had ever been. I was getting more respect than I had ever received. My world changed, and yours will too.

You are starting this journey at the perfect time. I'm lucky that I stumbled upon this stuff in my early 20's. While many young adults are approaching 30 confused and frustrated, I was focused. I knew who I was, where I was going, and I was doing everything necessary to get there. Call it positive thinking or the law of attraction, but everything just seemed to be working out.

The night of my 37th birthday, a buddy and I were talking about life. He is in his early 30's and loving life. We both believe the way you enter your 30's will make or break the rest of your life. The reason your 20's are the most important years of your life is because thriving in your 20's will position you for success in your 30's. You aren't going to enter "real adulthood" confused and frustrated. You're going to enter your 30's with confidence and momentum because you are living your life true to yourself.

A Leadership Mindset

I'm going to let you in on a little something that I didn't realize until I had been studying this for five or six years. As you are going through the steps and taking consistent action, what you're really studying and practicing is leadership.

You have invested time and energy understanding and articulating your values and passions. You've created a vision that is a reflection of your values and passions. You have set goals and created plans that align with your values, passions, and vision. You've thought about the impact you want to have on the world and the legacy you want to leave. And more importantly, you are taking action to make it a reality.

That is Leadership.

When we are focused, we will bust through the initial resistance period that comes with any big change. We are confident, have momentum, and are setting the example. People are noticing what we are doing. When you are in this state, you are a leader. Now, we may not see ourselves as a leader, but it's not necessarily how we see ourselves–it's how other people see us. Because people take notice and we set the example, we have the power and influence to inspire others to do the same. We are walking our talk and living life according to our terms, whether we are just leading ourselves, our family, or an organization of people.

Everything we have done up to this point will provide

a solid foundation for whatever else we choose to do in our lives. You will find the principles you have learned in the previous pages will be relevant to all your personal and professional endeavors in the future. But this is just the beginning of your journey. There is more to learn. When you are focused on the right things for the right reasons, things just seem to flow your way.

Taking Things to Another Level

Everything you have done so far should be the foundation for your future.

By now you know:

- Who you are
- What you want
- Where you are going
- How you are going to get there

That is leadership!

To close, I want to leave you with some additional thoughts on how you can take things to the next level and be a leader the world desperately needs.

Surround yourself with the right people.

"It's hard to soar with the eagles when you hoot with the owls." No doubt you've heard the old adage that we are an average of the five people we surround ourselves with. Who are you surrounded by, and do they contribute to or take away from your vision?

This is a big one! You need to have people in your life that understand what you are trying to do–people who encourage, support, and will challenge you if needed. If you're lucky, you have those people close to you, like parents or friends. If you don't have those people around you, you need to find them. Over the past 14 years, I've sought out and leaned on mentors, coaches, psychologists, teachers, professionals, and like-minded friends. The nice thing about having self-awareness and focus in your 20's is that there are so few of you that do and when you have it, other people notice and they want to help. Don't be afraid to seek out support and help. But, when you do, you better show up and follow through!

Get education and experience.

"The only place that success comes before work is in the dictionary." Some of you are going to realize that outside of your passion, you might have very little understanding of the subject area. That's OK, but if this is the case, you need to figure out how to close that gap to learn what you need to learn to put yourself in a position to achieve your vision. You do not want to be that person who talks about what they want and how they want life to be different, but is not willing to do anything to get it. Before you know it, you'll be 45 playing the "woulda, coulda, shoulda" game. I knew the only way my vision was going to become a reality was if I continued to self-study, got my degree, and gained skills that aligned with my vision.

Get involved.

Up to this point, everything you've read has been about personal leadership, or in other words, leading yourself. If you want to lead others, you better be walking your talk. If you ask my six-year-old son what leaders do, he will tell you that leaders make people better. For me, leadership is about understanding what's important, knowing big picture goals, taking the right action, and making everyone better in the process. Get involved in causes or groups or clubs that are important and excite you so you can exercise your interests and passions around other people. You will learn more about leadership by working with others toward a common goal than you ever will in a book. Reading is a great way to educate yourself, don't get me wrong, but it's the difference between reading a play book and running a play live, feeling what it's like to score or get knocked on your butt. Others will notice your desire to get involved and you'll earn their respect. You will build trust because you want to make the people around you better.

Find ways to give value.

Relationships are non-stop exchanges of value and you're either giving value or you're taking it. Give more value than you take! To give value you must understand the people you work with well enough to know what is meaningful to them. This means we need to figure out what is important to people and what excites them. When we understand these things we can connect with them meaningfully.

We all want to be around people we can count on and trust, and when you are focused on giving more value than you receive, you are showing everyone that it's not all about you and that you are paying attention to their needs. When giving value to others, a good place to start is to think about what is important to them and what they are passionate about. Do you see a theme here?

Find ways to lead.

If you are getting involved, taking action, and providing value, guess what? You are already leading! It's probable that the people around you see that as well. You could stop there, but I encourage you to look for more formal leadership opportunities. If you're involved in a non-profit or part of a young professional group, get on the board of the organization. You will have greater influence, responsibility, and visibility. The experience you will get and the connections you make will benefit you the rest of your life. I waited until I was 30 before I got involved in our local young professional group. Within four months I applied to be on the board and the next two years I served as VP of Professional Development. The following two years I served on the board of Young Variety, a children's charity. Today, I am active in providing value where I can to the CEO of Man-Up Iowa, an organization that teaches life skills and leadership development to at-risk teenage boys.

Make people around you better.

Leadership is not about power, it's about people. When you make people better, you become powerful. I talk a lot about the concept of "quality of life" with my clients. First, take ownership over your quality of life. You deserve a great quality of life, and so does everyone else. Second, think about how you impact the quality of life of other people, because you do have impact whether you know it or not. If you approach the world with the intention that you want to make the people around you better, you will.

If you want to be a leader, you must first lead yourself. It's a choice to be made; it doesn't just happen. Get involved, take action, and improve the lives of those around you. Inspire and encourage others to do the same!

CHAPTER 15

The Rest of the Story

I feel extremely fortunate for my life and the opportunities that the world provides. I'm focused and thriving and truly trying to set an example of what it means to be a leader. I love what I do. But, as I shared at the beginning, things weren't always like this. In the first chapter I talked about losing my first job out of college and suffering rejection from a dream job because of my attitude. The reality is, those events were part of a much bigger pattern.

I was a troubled kid; I grew up in a chaotic house with an alcoholic father and a mother doing her best to keep everything together for her family. My dad didn't just drink; he would drink, pass out, and wake up to wreak havoc on anyone who was around. When I was four or five years old, I remember watching him back my mom into corners while he yelled at her, calling her every foul name in the book. The experience of watching him throw my oldest sister through our hallway wall or the time he gave me a black eye for wanting to open a Christmas present early sticks with me today.

The older and bigger I became, the more I took on the role of protector. It wasn't uncommon for me to tackle him or toss him around in a fit of anger. He was always yelling, and most of the time I just wanted him to shut up. I was a sophomore in high school when things came to a head. One day after school, he got in my face and we were nose to nose. I can still smell the Black Velvet and Pepsi on his breath. He made a lot of threats to me over the years and this day was no different. He always used to tell me that I might get the best of him, but he would get his licks in. That day he decided to try, and punched me right in the face. As soon as he connected, I swung back and sent him crumbling to the ground. He didn't move. I thought I killed him. That was the last fight we ever had. Soon after that, with my mother's support, I kicked him out of the house. For the first time in my life we had peace. More importantly, my mom had peace.

If you look at the research on children who grow up in this type of environment, you realize there are some pretty troubling consequences during childhood and into adulthood. To this day I feel bad for everything my mother had to deal with. She didn't deserve it.

As a result of that environment, I was angry and misguided. Any young boy that doesn't develop a trusting relationship with their father or the man in their life is going to grow up with some issues. I was needy and constantly felt out of place. The perception of other people having the normal or perfect lives we didn't made me very insecure. I saw these well-behaved kids at school or church who took their studies seriously, and that was not me. As a result I was causing all kinds of trouble for myself and stress for my mother.

At four or five years old, I was getting chased up my driveway for throwing mud balls or snowballs at cars. As a six year old, I took my first ride in a police car for throwing rocks through windows at a nearby elementary school. I never cared about school and failed 6th grade. I only advanced to 7th grade because my mom made me change schools. At 14, I took my second ride in a police car when I was arrested for stealing baseball cards. Freshman year of high school I was academically ineligible to wrestle. When I finally was eligible, I got mad and quit halfway through my junior year. When I graduated high school, my cumulative GPA was 1.9, and on top of that, three months before graduation my girlfriend got pregnant. My daughter was born three weeks before my 19th birthday.

The birth of my daughter was a wakeup call that made me take life more seriously, but I was still operating with the same beliefs and attitude that kept me in survival mode. I was trying to follow "the plan," but was still an immature and misguided young man who grew up with very little leadership. After starting and quitting college twice, I finally stuck with it and completed my associate's degree that led to my position at the ad agency which fired me at my one year review.

I like to use this story when I speak to different audiences. When I talk to adults, I use it to build credibility and show right away that I walk my talk. When I speak to teens, I tell my story as if I am talking about some guy I know. When I finish I ask them what kind of man do they think he is? What do they think he is doing with his life? What kind of father do they think he is? The common responses are that he's probably in jail or has a crappy job and doesn't take care of his kid. They are always shocked and excited to hear that it was me. My hope is that they can use my story as an example of how life can be different when we are willing to focus on the right things. That's my hope for you too!

Everyone Has A Story

I used to think my situation was extreme, but the more I learn about other people, the more I realize that everyone has a story that impacts them today. I've also learned the impact our story has on us is largely dependent upon our attitudes and perceptions of ourselves and the world around us. Even though I was misguided as a kid, I knew at a very young age that I was never going treat my family the way my father did. Others grow up in the same environment only to repeat the cycle.

If your story is holding you back, this is your opportunity to change that. In chapter two, I talked about the negativity bias and why it's easy to feel sorry for ourselves and play the "woulda, coulda, shoulda" game. Stop it! Up to this point it has served you in some way, but you have to make the decision that it no longer serves you–that you want and deserve something more.

Own your story, don't let it own you!

This book is the result of my decision to own my story. Writing a book has been on my bucket list for over 10 years, but insecurity has always held me back. I've taken days off work to do nothing but write. I've written thousands and thousands of words only to save them in a folder somewhere. In June of 2014, I was on a plane from Minneapolis, Minnesota, to Las Vegas, Nevada, and I was listening to the audiobook *The Millionaire Messenger*, by Brendon Burchard. I can't tell you exactly what he said, but there was a section on being confident in your story and owning it. The message hit me like a bolt of lightning, and soon after we got in the air, I turned off the audiobook, opened my laptop, and started writing. By the time we landed in Vegas, I was done with chapter one.

What is it about your story that holds you back? In the columns below, reflect on your story and note the good, bad, and the ugly.

Made Me Stronger	Holds Me Back

The sooner you come to terms with the parts of your story that hold you back, the sooner you will get on the confident road, focusing on the right things for the right reasons, and moving in the direction you want to go. We change for two reasons; to avoid pain or pursue opportunity. When I was 23, I felt so much emotional pain that I couldn't take it any longer. Once I committed to changing my story, it didn't take very long before opportunity became my motivator. Make your story your greatest motivator.

Create the Meaningful Life You Deserve

You are in your 20's and sometimes you feel unstoppable, sometimes you're scared as hell, and sometimes you're just scared to fail and disappoint your loved ones. It's OK to admit that. Do you really know what the people in your life want for you? They want you to be confident, mentally and emotionally strong, and happy. They want you to find your passions and go after them. They want you to have a meaningful life.

My daughter was born three weeks before my 19th birthday. She has listened to me yap about this stuff since she was four years old. I remember having her captive in the backseat of my car, talking to her about values and character and choices. Today with all the craziness in the world and all the decisions she is going to have to make in the future, do you know what I want for her? I want her to live her life with confidence, have mental and emotional strength to face and overcome life's adversities, and to be happy. I want her to find her passions and make them happen. I want her to have a meaningful life.

This is your time to take control of the rest of your life. If you don't, you run the risk of falling victim to a world, culture, and system that has a long history of chewing people up and spitting them out. Take a look around you. How many people can you honestly say are living the lives they desire? You can. And if you take seriously what you've read in this book, you will. Remember, we're not talking about perfection. We're talking about a meaningful life.

The best thing that ever happened in my life is the gift I'm trying to give to you. If I can do it, you can do it!

I don't care who you are, where you come from, or what your background is.

I don't care how perfect or crappy your parents were.

I don't care how flawless your life has been or how many mistakes you've made.

I don't care whether or not you went to college or how much money you make.

I don't care how confident you think you are or what insecurities hold you back.

None of this stuff matters in the grand scheme of things. Some of it might make things a little easier or harder at times, but life is a marathon, not a sprint. It's not about quick success and superficial happiness. Life is about focusing on the right things for the right reasons and taking consistent action in the direction you want to be going.

It's your time to build a foundation that will serve you the rest of your life.

It's your time to take meaningful action in the direction you want to go.

It's your time to achieve meaningful results.

It's your time to get FOCUSED!

Notes

1. Retrieved December 20, 2014 at the *Oxford Dictionaries* website, http://www.oxforddictionaries.com/us/definition/american _english/identity-crisis

2. Gladwell, M. (2013) "Zeitgeist Americas 2013," Retrieved June 9, 2015 from *Lybio.net*, http://lybio.net/malcolm-gladwell-zeitgeist-americas-2013/science-technology

3. The TRACOM Corporation (2014) *Adaptive Mindset for Resiliency Concepts Guide*

4. Retrived March 15, 2015 at the Council of American Survey Research Organization website, https://www.casro.org

5. Zamora, S., "What Is Confidence, Really?" Retrieved December 20, 2014 at *HuffingtonPost.com,* http://www.huffingtonpost.com/ stephenie-zamora/meaning-of-confidence_b_3727675.html

6. Maslow, A. (1943) "A Theory of Human Motivation," Retrieved December 20, 2014 at website: *Classics in the History of Psychology*, http://psychclassics.yorku.ca/Maslow/motivation.htm

7. Covey, S., "The Seven Habits of Highly Effective People," Retrieved December 20, 2014 from *StevenCovey.com*, https://www.stephencovey.com/7habits/7habits-habit4.php

8. Clements, S., "Double Vision," Retrieved December 20, 2014 at *EMythBenchmark.com*, http://www.e-mythbenchmark.com/ business_coaching_tips/2013/11/double-vision.html

9. Covey, S., "The Seven Habits of Highly Effective People," Retrieved December 20, 2014 from *StevenCovey.com*, https://www.stephencovey.com/7habits/7habits-habit4.php

In addition to being an author,
Jason is a speaker, trainer, and coach!

Jason the Speaker

Some of Jason's audiences include leaders & managers, top achievers, young professionals, and college students. He speaks about the Success Skills of Confident Leadership, High-Performing Teams, Hiring with Purpose, Work Life Balance, and Unshakable Confidence.

Jason the Trainer

Jason works strategically with leaders across the nation in the areas of Strategic Planning, Self-Management, Relationship Building, Building High-Performing Teams, Coaching, and Resolving Conflict.

Jason the Coach

Jason works with individuals committed to being the best they can be. He takes clients through his six-to-nine month Success Skills program where they focus on their values, vision, and mastering Success Skills 1 and 2, Self-Management and Relationship Building

Jason's purpose is to inspire confidence in people. To learn more about Jason and how to work with him, please visit **www.JasonKiesau.com**

"This training was more than what I expected! It was absolutely the best leadership training I have ever attended; real life leadership training."

– Parc Communities' Leadership Team Member